POEMS FROM THE TURN AROUND

Poems by James P. McNamara

Kansas City   Spartan Press   Missouri

Spartan Press
Kansas City, Missouri
spartanpresskc.com

Copyright © James P. McNamara, 2019
Second Edition
ISBN: 978-1-950380-24-4
LCCN: 2019938175

Design, edits and layout: Jeanette Powers, Jason Ryberg, Jason Preu, Mike Clark
Cover and interior photos: James P. McNamara
All rights reserved. No part of this publication may be reproduced or transmitted in any form or by any means, electronic or mechanical, including photocopying, recording or by info retrieval system, without prior written permission from the autho

This book was originally part of the Spartan Press POP Poetry series, which ran from 2015 to 2017.

Table of Contents

Four Percent Chance of Rain / 1

Bobby Kennedy / 3

#4 / 5

All Catastrophe's Call / 6

Diet Plan / 7

#2 / 8

A Congress of Beasts / 9

Boy / 10

Dead City Initiatives / 11

Landing / 14

Descending Aspect / 15

#6 / 16

Divest / 17

Campaign Signs / 19

In Moments : Static / 20

Fumbling / 22

#3 / 24

Hanging Garden / 25

Half Speed / 26

Hangdog Myth / 27

Little Cause / 28

Songs in the Protectorates / 29

Storage / 30

Men of My Name / 32

#5 / 33

Company Dime / 34

Coward King of the Plains / 35

Ominous Portent / 38

Push Leaves / 39

Thewholetownhallgonerabidagain / 40

When It Is / 41

The Drummer's Sum Excerpt / 42

#7 / 43

Where the Money Went / 46

Learning to Sleep / 47

#8 / 49

Salad Days / 50

This Week in the Dead / 51

For Tara, Penelope, and Kansas City. All of whom,
should be considered co-author in my work.

*— Cloudy at the edges of a wider lense —
to enquire with the ingenuity of the exploited.
To apply your edges to the soft places
The only way you have left*

Four Percent Chance of Rain

What's left in me to leave unattended?
In the high noon,
to raw red in flooded light.

What sweetening latchkey
foam recedes as I face forward,
the woodwind drunk
that might bubble once and walk on.

The conditions are wilder beyond these windows
and permit no butterfats knowledge to balm,
but at moments they pause
and that is enough utility to begin.
I travel with tools.

A bag with a corner cut,
filled with crumbled
notes and pharmacy receipts.

Improving ape, buoyant for the time being
playing that meager percentage as mean.

There is a 4% chance of rain today
I stuff a jacket into my bag
pry the hole in the bag a little wider with a finger
and then my route:

a little trail of paper.

Bobby Kennedy

Bobby Kennedy wasn't real.
Exfoliating
the cure hardened ends
adding another layer to fresh meaning
the deft camera work preservation
> *The old film losing its color balance*
> *submerging slowly in ambient Jim Crow acid*
> *blistering white from temporary stained glass.*

succumbing
to the tart air invading the canisters.
His volumes.
The great white hope never made it to the ring.
It was lip sync service
to a tide shift.
He never left that shack.
He never exited translucent at the threshold:
sick, stammering.
> He never could know
> just how rain-proof his canopy was.

    Searching for sense
while the camera caught his profile
missing the layer of skin that had his cribbed notes.
Our figment saw the wood, heard the shift of dirt
crowding leather soles.
He almost could smell the moisture
become mud in dense Mississippi air.
But he never broke through.
Writhing through the grates
               to tangible in an almost era.
    He couldn't have been there
    the cornerstone at the shack
    Bobby Kennedy wasn't real.

#4

In defense of a hallowed secret namesake
the man was hung from the 3rd
story balcony: calculating the geometry
and physics of a recent
    blood panic immediacy.

The iron clad chain hooked into his clavicles
his words and whispers were spilling from
there, that and everything else.

That night we drink box wine
from the faux wooden thrift store bowls
and howl.

All Catastrophe's Call

All catastrophe's call
quietly dismissed
in the places less populous
forge bare economy from inevitable ends

    Bring bleached bones to pasture
aspirate the sand
irrigate the stone
in the land of plenty

Facility bound now and
hospital cloth disposable
Warned of flood, the bunks sag low
in preparation

    Old bedsprings threatening the
concrete with chalky scrapes

Diet Plan

I have changed diets.
I am on a new plan.
Feasting on Ted Cruz from a distance.

I absorb every frown and failure through my pores
: *Schadenfreude* osmosis
I sweat out his excess self assurance.

I will feast and feast and feast
until Ted's skin is paper, until the sun shines through him.

I will drink until his gelatin crystallizes,
until Ted's muscles are dried chiles
glued to a porous skeleton
     : delicate and hollow like a bird.

I will feast on Ted Cruz and then
bury his scarecrow in compost.
I will grow a tomato from it
     and feast on that too.

#2

2 girls in hijab feed birds
on a stone patio. Conversing softly,
prying fingers between the puffed folds of the loaves.
Wind tussled the ornate floral patterns burst from
the gray and brown stone.
The 1st Wednesday sirens whine
with a wide throat from the pole at their backs,
scaring away the birds. Who would be back,
but now it's just two girls in bright clothes
with a pile of half torn bread.

A Congress of Beasts

A congress of beasts
caught the virus.
Convulsing abdominal rocking.
Shouting down to the grass,
they stomp patches to path.
Hot with fever.
Want for water.
They stomped til it was paved
Mewling to the roots.
Pounding down the seeds.

The road expanded, unfurling like a tarp
                 — edges slapping at the air —
The beasts bones were crushed for chalk
and
lanes were made marked.

A nation of monsters
marched to war well after
across a smooth brown plane.

Boy

I like you just fine.
She truncated from steaming pots.
The boy was dismissed,
newly aware of things that haunt.

Dead City Initiatives

With brick wall set to scale
tire fire around back
Scanning lights
down her lanes

Harvesting tangled bezoars
    of middle class aggregate
Suicidal ideation
    by ticking degrees

The ones
going places scuff heels in echo
With shadow strides
in the shifting neighborhoods
Reset to the front foot
and spring to a kneel

The big box gets divvied up
Clean lines

and
glinting windows
Gentle curves
and
distant bells
a smooth ride on the rails

At the old witch piles of twine and twig
encasing copper wires
and
brick phone circuit boards
side eye sneers topping off the well of faith

They'll scale that wall
to see signs of the peak
and the other end's descent
standing on the shoulders of giants
standing on the shoulders of a
    day
laborer pyramid

They'll cross that bridge
knock the fucker down
and name it for the bricklayer
in smirking reverence: the ironic wink

Who got what deal
and
what deal got who?

For just one eye dropper of temporary confirmation
they will self actualize and feast
They
us
in the blind spot colonies
nourished on viral etiquettes

Landing

I fell down a flight of stairs
Center of gravity
  shifted to a head full of dice games and 5% bottles
When I awoke my perspective shifted to the passive
The full weight of this
      full flight of stairs
           landed on top of me
The world itself turned upside and threw my own home at me
    — I only woke my wife —

Descending Aspect

-for Neil Goss

The rendering fat totem
scales a bare fertile thread
Baked in earth to soften,
musculature enveloping looping hollow bone
Hanging smells of dirt and city nothing
Somewherebetween
exhaust and stale concrete
A bloom digs out
Swollen summer flies cling like heat
policing the periphery of
design It's to us to
build a house to burn it down:
supporting the vine that grips
to be cons umed while
replenishing the
descending
aspect

#6

They kissed shortly,
but were two fists knuckle to knuckle.
There, sweetly,
was a challenge under the
umbrella skeleton sculpture.

Pausing to hold each other
and
make eye contact,
then to kiss again with darts.

That same belly fishing impact
in front of the murals on the abandoned shops.

In the same bald sun a man slept,
sweating on a duffel bag that was leaning
on the scalloped retaining wall.

Just a few feet away.

Divest

Bring blade and brick to wager
place them to the scales
listening for the scrape of the brick
as it flakes against brushed steel
offsetting the bell decagram on decagram

Bring flame to the gut
suppress its gravitational defiance
scald it back into periphery
look on

In the stillness before flint strikes
a brief congress with agency
surges behind the void
compression in the chest excavating winds of bravery
the cavity clenched
with steady milliliters of warm ancestral data

evaluating threats in shaken brush
and baton beat marching drums
Let us fabricate the wilds, scavenge for teeth
Collect fallen bones, scatter them at your doorstep

Bind two twigs for effigy
Bind two more for protection

Carve wider corners in
meters
from the rustling hunting grounds

We can hear it in the pulverized glass on the paved hills

We can see it when hands go up against mundane skies

We can feel it in the in the forced
climb of shirt buttons on our uniforms

We have built our finest predator
given right to eat the black young corralled
to extort hours from mayflies

fountains of pathology equations
with only the pressure to refill its own scrying pool

the untamed, divest of these scales
and bring bits to burn as they rediscover the science of fire

Campaign Signs

Tomorrow,
we let the wind take
    down the campaign signs,
but, tonight
tonight is for pleas behind podiums
platitudes broad-shouldering the close up.
Percentages reporting

clenched fists working for field goal distance
reminiscing on
the food and sex of futility.

In Moments : Static

The words dissolve faster than ever
bobbing
heads above the breach
and receeding.
Taking in one and only breath
a deep gulp of mist.

But you are not dead
yet and
still have your hard soles from
concrete summers:
barefoot ball on rubble streets.

You are not dead
yet and
still have feeling in your fingertips from
gliding them across
the skin of another.

Into the depths of
the little villages
dragging callous, scuffles into toddling
breakneck grammar
and walled garden thoroughfares
we dive.

Hold your chin out
sturdy as a stormcloud appears
watch the extracted syntax
Paint the screens around you. Stand awhile.

You are not dead
yet and
still, though uglied up a bit, can dig and swim.

Fumbling

Running our fingers
against your cavernous veins,
barefoot and sinking to the ankle.

Warmly
eroding when the floods come
in bits like bread in ponds.

We trickle into your cake earth
still-as-ever current dissolving into
root systems.

We feel our way down, beloved.
Grasping in your thin vacuum,
your fresh moisture clings to our backs.

We, caravan in your anthills,
lightless,
following only rhythm pulse.

Push on deeper,
until deeply
we are the blood.

#3

She swept and made the coffee.
Wobbling slightly
around the grounds and dust and over the broom
she said

have a good one, sugar puddin.

And sugar began as a shush that quickly,
it dragged the *urrr* in clumps from a
               pocket behind her tongue,
                       off to the side a little bit.

She then swept some more.

Hanging Garden

The damp vegetation packed tight in the gutters,
clinging loosely to the awning.
interwoven coppers and browns,
white paint reaching the last season of its resistance.
What will be flowers began to bloom this morning.
Green little stalks lazily stretching,
threatening to bud, in a hanging garden
bowing the corrugated tin planter.
screws straining from the winter weight.
Weeds and flowers yawning to a greening sky with quick wispy clouds.
Even when you do nothing something happens.
Just ask my landlord.

Half Speed

Poems to shout at
half speed
        reduced 2 sounds
Until repeated
Us each, in a throng
Us each, given a syllable
to shout until they come together
it will come together
        once.
Then we walk away

Hangdog Myth

Placing a palm to your sternum,
pushing through your hard plates,
shifting into the fat and caul
to gently cradle your hangdog myth
&
brush fingertips across the wrinkles,
teasingly pinch the paper thin valves.
It jumps.
Resist the urge to pop it.
To bite in with fingernail and
feel the pulps, flaky sugars and acids, dribble
down my wrist and dry to me.

Little Cause

She had little cause for faith
and less cause for promise.
When I said I was done
and was done and meant it for the dozenth.
Faith was not the coal or the copper
nowhere to conduct and nothing burn
she had only the
wait-and-see.

Maybe this time was a story
for another woman in another era who
hadn't built the case for another *yes* just yet.
We had been simultaneous carpenters
for some time.
I had been digging around her posts.
She was framing the second floor.

Wait and See
and here we are.

Songs in the Protectorates

Fading language songs
from the *That Part Of Town* protectorate
float like dandelion puffs.
They cram into the dead-end alleyways.
They crowd
and pack
and clog
until they spill out around the corners.

And like that
a windows closes or a car shuts off.
                        Gone like someone
                            pulled a
                                plug.

Storage

As expected:
aspirations gathering dust
in the warehouse floor plan.

Angular window seats
in the innovation echo chamber,
where they clipped addendums to the line.

Utopias piled to the ceiling
in a corner somewhere.
Schematics,
    blueprints,
        doctrines, and
   scale models of better tomorrows water damaged.

There are tears in the solar sails on shelf 38b
and
some short timer spilled paint on the suborbital public housing
      initiative.

A collection of Tankie grad students
25 point plans for cultural revolution
is due for incineration this month,
gotta make room for the incoming tech bubble
     C h e a t c o d e s.

The gray white tones of sneaking sun rises
shuffle through the sawdust.

It's hard not to notice that the footprints
are to the bathroom,
the coffee pot,
and then back to desks.

No one bothers with
caution tape anymore
    and they
stopped keeping records years ago.

Men of My Name

The bottles follow the men of my name
tied to our belts with ribbons or yarn
    we forage from the ground.
The bottles scrape concrete with our steps
knocking into each other, tangling into knots.
They roll to a stop when we tie another.
We then
drop our new feather of wedding luck
and lurch forward.

At times
the wind catches the necks
and they sing briefly...

The men of my name
    dragging occasional chimes.

#5

He watches turkish sitcoms on his phone at the counter,
I don't know what they are saying
but the rhythm of a joke is the rhythm of a joke.
And when you don't know?
There's laughter as punctuation.
And it's there,
female voices feign shock and tumble to the get
— they speak with pace / chimes in storm —
a choral harmony.
The laughter lands like a bullet
and shakes loose the moment,
fading out
sifting the eyes and ears
through that final grate:
a fine powder journey to forget.

He chuckles, eating kifta,
the bartender silently refills his water.

Company Dime

Productivity, in fact. Possibly disruption, if you must.
The windows are open.
    Sun yellowed clump of air just out of
reach. Clacking and shoveling
for someone else who is doing the same
but less for someone else
    and up the chain to the window seat.
Sweeping away down here on ground level.
When you can   and especially
when you shouldn't:
idle with great diligence and care.

Torpor like one cuts diamonds.

    Give heed to no warnings of time
wasted
if that time is yours indeed.

Coward King of the Plains

The Coward King of the Plains
sits on a fainting couch throne
of impact foam and bubble wrap
murmuring soft theocracy

Practicing a brave face in a hand mirror
his caution tape crown slides down his brow

The looming threat of dark-skinned children
dragging shadows of darker circumstances approaches
He must be diligent

He checks his posture for the cameras

The Coward King of the Plains
don't go outside no more
he sits behind his telescope
wrapped in a blanket he got on vacation in braver days
before his reality congealed into quavering cubes

He can no longer hear his own dog whistles

He peeks through his blinds
loading his pistols
as the headlights pass his driveway
The Coward King will live through this night

The Coward King of the Plains
straps into his five point harness in his limo
He looks out tinted windows
gently patting the black steel of the roll cage
He forgot something at the grocery store

The Coward King of the Plains
shoots awake
sweating.
More dreams of widows on the march
followed by welfare queen escalade tanks
blaring deep bass tones
shatters the bullet proof glass on his podium

The judges cornered
the teachers flee

the ATM's drain 25 bucks at a time
with a line around the block
Soon will families uproot
and the textbooks will decay
He'll never ask the question
about the people in his petri dish

The Coward King peeks
from beneath his ghillie suit sitting perfectly still
Sliding his camera phone under the bathroom stall
That young man had very full hips
and you can never be too safe these days

He shaves his face for 45 minutes at a time
one inch at a time
with pauses to catch his breath
wheezing his mantra
If it breaks it's because it always does. No maintenance needed.

This is how the Coward King begins the day in his high tower.
Long may he reign.

Ominous Portent

The airline bottle was just where I left it.
Behind the bleach,
under the sink.

This foreshadows nothing.

Inserting its palms between the subcutaneiae in my belly,
spreading its fingers to a slow grip.
The fingers move as snakes on stone,
beginning a long slow homecoming,
tingling salivation where my jaw meets throat.

These will vanish.
This is steam from a pot.

Push Leaves

The plains wind can barely push leaves
                it can barely push leaves

It is the scent on our skin
the bald tire skitting stink and a
clutch of trees
aligning, without redress, the trafficway curves
The thrift store walmart music bone abrasion that
finds your gaps: that calcifies

It's the teeth marks on our necks
dangerously close to the ears
a row of little dips:
the nipping sex ritual of fading
We've never seen our heroes here
and that is our
little magic to muster
though it can barely push leaves

Thewholetownhallgonerabidagain

Only shambling jaws,
                snapping.
Feet flat and clapping the roar rises like
the hum beneath the floorboards
vibrating skulls at their where-the-spine-meets.
Gentle euphoria wide mouthed with cracked teeth.
The vacuum breaks as the vents kick on:
                hoof rolls
           in the corridors.
Dancing to the organ downbeats. Clacking linoleum,
the musical spine
of bloating exaltations float
for the rending.
The whole townhall gone rabid again.
The grain of the meat to run the edge across
ragged. Then
exposed texture and tossed
aside.
Cut only to be cut   and little else.
Typical selves, it's
                typical.

When It Is

When it is she and I,
her lips envelop sturdy tones that
   shake into me,
humming through my spine, belly and joints.
   It is her sight.
She speaks in sonograms to me when the lamp chain
is last tugged.
We,
when it is uninterrupted.

The Drummer's Sum Excerpt

With lithesome fealties
on shifting ladder rungs / momma went to night school
and woke before the sun

#7

He walked up,
gray hard hairs,
thinning at the top
evaporating at his shoulders.
He stopped.
Swaying in school boy blue shorts,
like there was music enfolding him,
just for him (maybe there is).
Orange tie dye shirt craggy at the belt-line from hard sleep.
Duffel bag, stuffed.

Hey, brotherman you got any change?
Nah. Sorry, man.
I shrugged. He looked past me and around the park.
Got a smoke? he asked pleasantly.
Oh, sure.
I fish for my pack.
... and a lighter?
I got so fucked up last night I lost it.

He laughed a little laugh inward
from the top of his chest,
collapsing in his throat.

Been there, man.
He swayed slowly
in his private theater.
He peeled the filter loose
from the smoke with a pinch of the
forefinger and thumb,
clamping the lighter with his pinkie.
Too weak this way as he tossed the filter
to nowhere in particular *need it to burn* he
laughed into his throat.

The left side of his smile
was browned and beaten,
tanned like a used coffee cup.
Yeah, he started. He stared past me.
... *I know people got lives and they* ... Words retreated him,
into the interior hope. Dropping for a moment.

My name's Adam, man. It was real nice to meet you.

He pulled back out. I told him the same that he told me.
I saw him two days later through a window,
same shirt wrinkled at the waist.
He swayed through the crosswalk mob,
one day he will sway
to the other side of this.
All the way through.

Where the Money Went

The water main popped
bleeding
out from beneath
pooling in the years cracked
and punctured alleyways

rallying in uneven
gutters
sagging alongside decaying tar
illuminating
where the money went

Learning to Sleep

No longer of the unknown hours
and alleyway short cuts
not of the memorized path
No trundling through the
empty places between squatting plum bricks
awash
in the piecemeal constructed dusk around the corner
the cold copper pink lamplight from days of industry
Feet
clopping knowing your shadow only
as it pushed a barrier to the others encroaching
Erected
apex predator
through an arched spine
(eyes beneath the hood)
After the revelers went to echo behind
the empty city
and the bus stop sleepers

the crosswalk a full block wide
and movement was untethered
but daylight has gentled
and that lie no longer holds
now, learning to sleep
without sirens and distant trains

Make amends with it
Give it the time to caress you
Let it guide you
grip you by the ribs
and compress the diaphragm
tracing your abdominal muscles
hitching a ride on the sighs you expel
Deeply now and breathe back in
catch it before it drifts too far
It has this home in you
Bend like this
and know

#8

The Pallet Truck idled, shaking from the axles.
It was with walls on its bed.
4 unique collections of goods,
puzzled together in a fashion that
intimates practiced ease, like knots on a sailboat
The buckets strapped down filled with cables,
the shims bundled.
The framework and ropes
and ladders.
They 3 in highlighter yellow vests,
dingy white henley's and gray hoodies, hardhats,
cigarettes dangle from their lips
and they pace around
or drape their arms
on signposts, on the truck in enviable ease
and it's early yet,
the sunlight is merely a threat around the corner,
a block away.
The tie straps fly free
in wide tall arcs and hit the
concrete flat like a dead bird.

Salad Days

Shuffle through the flashes,
when you found the floor again.
The abrupt achilles aware shock.
The regurgitated proof of the moment.
The *Ope* of it outloud.
You were in line
at the grocery store and you
had the book and so many were waiting
and you wished it weren't so many
but it was and so many more.
When you were ceased,
when the real neural meat of you began to pulse.
The narrowness of it unfettered
to every other insistence,
and in the God's honest daylight of it,
patting down daylight that went missing,
you had to get both
gallons of milk to get the bread.

Hook a line to luck that comes with a look over the shoulder.

This Week in the Dead

This week in the dead: nothing much to report.
Still as ever current;
bearing the load of a needling anxiety,
— The final subdermal rake chasing us from ear to ear.
The torrents beneath sleep. —

Still as ever current; trickling into cake earth.

Goodnight.

www.ingramcontent.com/pod-product-compliance
Lightning Source LLC
Chambersburg PA
CBHW030133100526
44591CB00009B/637